Four volume edition 1986.

volume **3**

BIG BIRD'S
SESAME STREET
DICTIONARY

FEATURING JIM HENSON'S SESAME STREET MUPPETS

LETTERS L–Q

by Linda Hayward

illustrated by Joe Mathieu

Editor in Chief: Sharon Lerner

Art Directors: Grace Clarke and Cathy Goldsmith
with special thanks to Judith M. Leary

Funk & Wagnalls, Inc./Children's Television Workshop

Ll

A B C D E F G H I J K **L** M N O P Q R S T U V W X Y Z

ladder A ladder is something that you can climb to reach high places. A ladder has steps that are called rungs.

Fire fighter Ernie is climbing a **ladder.**

lake A lake is water with land all around it. A lake is larger than a pond.

Prairie Dawn is paddling her canoe on the **lake.**

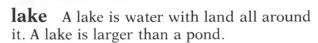

land Land is the part of the earth that is not water. Another word for land is ground.

I can travel on **land**…

On water…

And in the air.

land When something lands, it comes down to the ground.

Grover's airplane is going to **land.**

language   Language is what we use to say things to other people. When two people understand each other's words, they know the same language.

Cookie Monster can say COOKIE in five different **languages.**

Cookie
(English).

Biscuit
(French).

Galleta
(Spanish).

Biscotto
(Italian).

餅乾

Bǐng gān
(Chinese).

large   Large means big.

Marshal Grover ordered a small glass of milk for himself and a **large** glass of milk for Fred.

last   When something is last, it comes after all the others.

Cookie Monster is the **last** in line. He wishes he were first.

late   When you are late, you come after the time that you were supposed to.

You're **late** for our party, Connie!

I'm sorry. I couldn't find my broom.

HAPPY HALLOWEEN

late   Late can also mean near the end.

The party ended **late** at night. Everyone had a good time.

later   Later means after now.

Hey, Bert! Do you want a banana?

Later, Ernie! Right now I'm busy working on my bottle cap collection.

laugh When you laugh, your whole face smiles and you make ha-ha sounds.

laundry Laundry is all the clothes that need to be washed or the clothes that have just been washed.

Ernie and Bert are doing their **laundry.**

lay When you lay something down, you put it down.

Bart **laid** his cards on the table.

lazy Someone who is lazy does not want to work or to play.

The cat and the pig and the mouse are **lazy.**

lead When you lead, you show others the way by going with them or in front of them.

leader A leader is someone who leads.

leaf A leaf is a thin, flat green part of a tree or a plant. It grows at the end of a branch or a stem.

learn When you learn, you find out something that you did not know before.

*I had to **learn** to use a lasso.*

*I am **learning** how to use a lasso, too.*

*I have a lot more to **learn**.*

leave When you leave, you go away.

When you leave something behind, it does not go with you.

When you leave something alone, you do not touch it or bother it.

*Come on, Ernie. It's time to **leave** for the show.*

*Do you think we should **leave** these cookies here?*

__Leave__ them alone, Ernie. We don't have time to put them away.

LATER

left When something is left, it is still there after all the others are gone.

Cookie Monster ate almost all of the cookies. There is only one **left**.

left Left is also a direction. It is the opposite of right.

*Now let me see. Should I turn **left** or right?*

If I were Goldilocks, I would turn around and go home.

HOUSE of the THREE BEARS

HOUSE of the BIG BAD WOLF

LEFT

RIGHT

leg   Your leg is the part of your body between your hip and your foot. Look up the word body.

Bert's **legs** are longer than Ernie's **legs.**

> Ernie, I think you are wearing my pants.

length   The length of something is how long it is from one end to the other.

> The **length** of this straw is eight inches.

> The **length** of a story is its number of pages or how much time is needed to read or tell it.

Look up the word inch.

less   Less means not as much.

> I have **less** milk than Bart has.

> I have the **least** amount of milk.

let   When you let something happen, you allow it to happen.

> **Let** the balloon fly away!

> Okay. I **let** it go.

letter   A letter is a mark that stands for a sound. There are twenty-six letters in the alphabet. You can put letters together to make words. Look up the word alphabet.

letter   A letter is also a message that you write on paper and give or mail to someone.

> I, the Amazing Mumford, will now pull from this perfectly empty hat two different things that have the same name.

> A LA PEANUT BUTTER SANDWICHES!

librarian A librarian is someone who works in a library.

library A library is a room or building where books are kept. You can borrow books from a library.

Farley went to the **library.** The **librarian** helped him find a book about dragons.

lick When you lick something, you touch it or taste it with your tongue.

Lasso Louise likes to **lick** luscious lollipops.

Say that ten times, fast.

lid A lid is a cover.

The **lid** to Oscar's garbage can is on his head.

lie When you lie, you rest on your stomach or back or side.

Barkley likes to **lie** near Big Bird's nest.

lie A lie is something that is not true.

Hey, Bert, there's a big ugly monster with two heads and four arms and eight legs, and he's standing right behind you.

You can't scare me, Ernie. I know that's a big **lie.**

Gee, Bert, how did you know I wasn't telling the truth?

Because the monster is standing behind *you*, not me!

lift When you lift something, you pick it up.

Herry Monster can **lift** a crane.

A crane can **lift** Herry Monster.

light When there is light, it is not dark and you can see. Something that gives light is sometimes called a light.

In the daytime, the sun gives us **light.**

At night, when it is dark, we can turn on electric **lights.**

light When you light something, you set it on fire.

Mommy, after you **light** the candles on my birthday cake, I will blow them out.

Make a wish first, dear.

light When something is light, it is not heavy.

A feather is **light.** It is easy to carry.

A big rock is heavy. It is not easy to carry.

lightning

Lightning is a flash of light you see in the sky.

Sometimes there is **lightning** during a rainstorm.

BOOM!

1 … one bolt of **lightning**!

like

When you like someone or something, that person or thing makes you feel good.

I really **like** Rubber Duckie.

like

When one thing is like another thing, they are the same in some way.

What is **like** a big red furry monster with horns?

Another big red furry monster with horns!

line

A line is a long, thin mark.

Lines can be straight or curved or wiggly or crooked.

line

When people or things are in a line, they are behind or next to each other. They are in a row.

There is a **line** of people waiting to see the new movie.

TICKETS

lion

A lion is a big, wild cat that roars.

I am a baby **lion.** I am a cub.

I am the cub's mother. I am a **lion**ess.

I am the cub's father. I am a **lion.**

A group of **lions** is called a pride. Grown-up male **lions** have manes. **Lion**esses do not.

14

BERT THE LION TAMER

Bert the lion tamer has lost his lion. Help Bert find his lion by finding the right path through the maze.

ENTER

Hint: Find the things beginning with the letter **L.**

liquid A liquid is something that is wet and can be poured.

Three of these things belong together. One of these things is not the same.

Orange juice, milk, and water are all kinds of **liquids.** A loaf of bread is not wet and cannot be poured.
The loaf of bread does not belong.

listen When you listen, you pay attention to the sounds you hear.

Hey, everyone! **Listen** to Little Jerry and the Monotones.

little Something that is little needs less room than something that is big. It is small, not large.

How do you become a big hairy monster?

You start out as a **little** hairy monster—and then you grow!

live To live somewhere means to have your home in that place.

I **live** in a garbage can. Slimey **lives** in a box. We both **live** on Sesame Street.

lock A lock is something that keeps something else from being opened. You usually need a key to open a lock.

lock When you lock something, you fasten it with a lock.

Sherlock Hemlock always **locks** his trunk with a big **lock.**

lonely When you feel lonely, you wish you had someone to be with.

It's **lonely** at the top.

long When something is long, the beginning is far from the end.

When something takes a long time, there is a lot of time between the beginning and the end.

It took me a **long** time to learn to use my lasso.

Lasso Louise has a **long** lasso.

look When you look, you pay attention to the things you see.

A detective has to **look** for clues.

loose When something is loose, it is not tight.

Farley put on his father's shoes. They are **loose.**

lose When you lose something, you cannot find it.

Did you **lose** something, Big Bird?

Yes, I **lost** the key to this lock.

I, Sherlock Hemlock, the world's greatest detective, will find the key with my trusty magnifying glass.

But first I must find my trusty magnifying glass. Where did I put that thing?

Did you **lose** it?

lost When something is lost, you cannot find it.

LOST AND FOUND DEPT.

LOST: one key to Big Bird's lock and one trusty magnifying glass

loud When something is loud, it makes a lot of sound.

That's too **loud**, Oscar!

What?

BANG!

BANG!

I said, THAT'S TOO **LOUD**, OSCAR!

If you'd stop yelling, Betty Lou, we could have some peace and quiet around here.

love When you love someone, you care about that person very much.

I **love** you, Mommy.

I **love** you, too, Grover, dear.

Sometimes when you like something very much, you say you **love** it.

I just **love** carrots.

low Something that is low is close to the ground.

I am flying high.

I am flying **low**.

Whoops! I am flying too **low**.

lunch Lunch is the meal that you eat in the middle of the day.

Biff and Sully are going to eat **lunch**. Biff's **lunch**box is empty.

I thought I saw something blue and furry with funny eyes go by.

One of my favorite L words is litter. I like litter because litter is trash.

Mm

A B C D E F G H I J K L **M** N O P Q R S T U V W X Y Z

machine Machines are built by people to do special kinds of work.

This **machine** makes mud.

DIRT 100% PURE

I'm **mad.** I'm really **mad.**

mad When you are mad, you do not like what has happened. You are angry.

magic Magic is a way of doing something that seems to be impossible. Magicians, witches, and fairies use magic to make amazing things happen.

Amazing Mumford the **magician** does **magic** tricks.

I, the Amazing Mumford, will make this monster disappear.

A LA PEANUT BUTTER SANDWICHES!

That is **magic!**

mail Mail is the letters and packages that are sent from one place to another.

Big Bird is dropping his **mail** into the **mail**box.

The **mail** carrier is putting the **mail** into his **mail**bag.

The **mail** carrier is delivering the **mail** to Granny Bird.

make Make means to put together or cause something to happen.

Cookie Monster loves to **make** cookies. Today he **made** twelve cookies and one mess.

make-believe When something is make-believe, it is imaginary. It is not real.

We are not real bears. We are only **make-believe**.

THE SESAME STREET PLAYERS GOLDILOCKS AND THE 3 BEARS

man A man is a grown-up boy.

There is one **man** in the elevator.

many Many means a lot of people, things, or animals.

There are **many** monsters in the elevator.

map A map is a special kind of picture that shows where places are.

This is a **map** of Sesame Street.

This is a **map** of the United States.

march When you march, you walk with rhythm in steps of the same size.

I want to see the Monster **Marching** Band **march** down Sesame Street.

mark A mark is a line, spot, dent, or sign on something. A mark can be made by accident or on purpose.

I made a **mark** on the map to show where we live.

Ernie, who made this crayon **mark** on our new table?

marry When two people marry, they become husband and wife.

The monsters are getting **married.**

Will you **marry** me?

Why not?

I now pronounce you husband and wife.

I just love weddings!

mask A mask is something you wear over your face.

Farley and Betty Lou are wearing **masks.**

Trick or treat!

match A match is a thin stick with a special end that is used to make a flame.

I never play with **matches. Matches** can be dangerous.

match When two things match, they are the same in a certain way.

THE MATCHING GAME!

And now folks, it's time for— THE **MATCHING** GAME! Each one of our contestants is holding a shape. All you have to do is find the shapes that **match.**

may May means allowed to.

maybe Maybe means possibly.

me Me is a word you use when you are talking or thinking about yourself.

meal A meal is all the food that is served when it is time to eat. You usually eat three meals a day—breakfast, lunch, and dinner.

mean When someone is mean, that person does or says things that are not kind or friendly.

mean What you mean is what you want to show by your words or your actions.

measure When you measure something, you find out how long or how heavy or how much it is.

I can **measure** my height.

I can **measure** my weight.

I can **measure** a cup of flour for baking cookies.

FLOUR

mechanic A mechanic is someone who uses tools to make or repair machines. Look up the word tool.

The Count's car is broken. The **mechanic** is trying to fix it.

medicine When you are sick, you sometimes use medicine to make you well.

Take your **medicine,** dear, like a good monster!

meet When you meet someone, you get together with that person.

I'm happy to **meet** you.

melt When something melts, it turns to liquid.

It is a warm day. The snow monster is starting to **melt**.

mess When things are dirty or out of place, we say they are a mess. When something is a mess, it is not neat.

I don't know anyone who can make a bigger **mess** than you, Oscar.

Gee thanks, Betty Lou. That's the nicest thing you've ever said to me.

metal   Metal is the hard stuff that some things are made of. Iron, gold, silver, and tin are kinds of metal.

Keys are made of **metal.**   Coins are made of **metal.**   Cans are made of **metal.**

middle   The middle is the place between the beginning and the end. The middle is also the place that is the same distance from all the sides. It is the center.

Three people are standing at the milk bar. Marshal Grover is in the **middle.**

Big Bird drew a circle with chalk. Little Bird is standing in the **middle.**

midnight   Midnight is twelve o'clock at night.

Dum de dum de dum. Time for my **midnight** snack!

milk   Milk is a liquid food that comes from cows and other animals. Milk is good to drink.

Farmer Grover's pail is full of **milk.** He has just **milked** his cow.

mind Your mind thinks and knows and remembers and feels.

Everyone at the bus stop is thinking of something different.
Three different **minds** are thinking three different thoughts.

To **mind** means to care.

Do you **mind** if I borrow your dictionary?

mine Mine means belonging to me.

This towel is yours. The other towel is **mine.**

minus Minus means take away or subtract.

$$3-1=2$$

Three **minus** one is two.

minute A minute is a small amount of time. There are sixty seconds in a minute. There are sixty minutes in an hour.

Waiter, you have exactly one **minute** to bring my milk.

Whoa, Bossie!

mirror A mirror is a glass in which you can see yourself.

Egad! A suspicious-looking person! I wonder who he is.

Sherlock, that is *you* in the **mirror.**

miss When you miss something, you do not hit it or find it or meet it or see it or hear it.

Keep your eye on the ball, Ernie, or you'll **miss** it.

Hurry, Sherlock, or you will **miss** the train.

I can't leave now. I'm looking for my **missing** ticket.

miss When you miss someone, you feel sorry that person is not with you.

What's the matter, Big Bird?

I **miss** Mr. Snuffle-upagus.

mistake When you make a mistake, you do something wrong.

I think we made a **mistake,** Sully.

mitten A mitten is a cover for your hand to keep it warm. A mitten has a place for your thumb and a place for your other fingers.

Farley is wearing red **mittens.**

mix When you mix things, you put them together.

You **mix** the potion while I read the recipe. Let's see... two toadstools, three bat wings...

The Count counts his money.

Can you count your money?

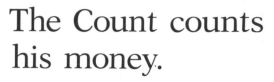

 penny
1 cent

 nickel
5 cents

 dime
10 cents

quarter
25 cents

half dollar
50 cents

one dollar
100 cents

10 = 2 = 1

25 = 5 = 1

50 = 10 = 5 =

2 = 1

100 = 20 = 10 =

4 = 2 =

money   Money is what we use to buy things.

Hey, kid. Would you like to buy an M? It costs only nine cents.

I don't have enough **money**. I have only six cents.

You're in luck. That's exactly what this wonderful W costs.

monkey   A monkey is a hairy animal with two arms and two legs. Most monkeys have long tails.

Do you know what is more fun than a barrel of **monkeys**?

Counting the **monkeys** in a barrel!

monster   A monster is a large or strange living thing.

The **monsters** on Sesame Street are furry and friendly.

month   A month is an amount of time that lasts about thirty days. There are twelve months in a year. Each month has a special name.

Thirty days hath September,
April, June, and November.
All the rest have thirty-one,
Excepting February alone,
And that has twenty-eight days clear,
And twenty-nine in each leap year.

moon   The moon is the earth's closest neighbor in space. You can sometimes see it in the sky.

Isn't the **moon** beautiful?

Grover the astronaut is on the **moon**.

Isn't the earth beautiful?

mop   A mop is made of yarn or sponge that is fastened to a long stick. A mop is used for cleaning floors.

Bert is using a **mop** to **mop** the floor.

more   More means a larger amount.

You have **more** cookies than I do, Ernie.

That's true, Bert. But Cookie Monster has **more** cookies than *I* do. He has the **most.**

morning   The morning is the first part of the day.

RING!

Oh! Time for my **morning** snack.

mother   A mother is a woman who has a child.

Grover's **mother** is reading a bedtime story to Grover.

Once upon a time…

SUPER GROV

motor   A motor is an engine.

Grover Knover's **motor**cycle has a **motor.**

mountain   A mountain is a part of the earth that is higher than the land around it.

I, Grover Knover, am climbing this very high **mountain.** Why? Because it is here.

mouse   A mouse is a small, furry animal with a long tail.

If you have one **mouse**…

And someone gives you another **mouse**…

You have two **mice.**

mouth   Your mouth is a part of your face. You eat, drink, and speak through your mouth. Look up the word face.

Hello, everybod-ee! I am here to tell you about the **mouth.** I am using my **mouth** to talk.

move   When you move, you go from one place to another place.

When you move something, you take it from one place to another place.

Sometimes the word move is used to mean changing the place where you live.

The **movers** are **moving** the country mouse to the city.

I think I'd like to **move** to the city.

CHEEZY MOVERS INC.

Ernie, let's **move** to another seat. I can't see the movie.

Prairie, please **move** your coat so I can sit in that seat.

That's not my coat. It's Cookie Monster sleeping.

ZZ

movie   A movie is moving pictures that you watch on a screen. A movie usually tells a story.

Bert and Ernie are watching a **movie.**

much   Much means a great amount.

THE SESAME STREET THEATER

NOW PLAYING

THE COUNTRY MOUSE MOVES TO THE CITY

Did you like the **movie,** Bert?

I liked it very **much.**

EXIT

mud   Mud is soft, wet dirt.

Who stepped in my box of **mud**?

Don't worry, Oscar. I will solve the mystery. I will look for someone with **muddy** shoes.

FRESH MUD

muscle   A muscle is a part of your body that can stretch and pull tight to make your body move. You have many muscles inside your body.

Herry Monster uses his **muscles** to lift the barbell.

music Music is pleasing sound that is played or sung by people. Different people like different kinds of music.

Everyone at the party is listening to the **music**.

Stop making that terrible noise!

Terrible noise? This is **music** to my ears.

must Must means have to.

I **must** find the person who is wearing muddy shoes. Then I will know who stepped in Oscar's mud box.

my My is another way of saying belonging to me.

Egad! **My** shoes are covered with mud. *I* am the person who is wearing muddy shoes.

I'll just sit down here and clean them off.

myself Myself is a word that is sometimes used instead of me or I.

mystery A mystery is something that you do not understand and try to figure out.

I found the mud on my shoes. I, **myself,** am the one who stepped in your mud box, Oscar. The **mystery** is solved.

Good, because I have another **mystery** for you to solve. Someone *sat* in my mud box.

Some of my favorite M words are missing from this dictionary— messy, moldy, and mushy. Do you know what I wish? I wish *I* were missing from this dictionary.

The MYSTERY OF THE MISSING MAGIC MICE

Mumford the magician
has lost his
22 magic mice.
Can you find them?

ABCDEFGHIJKLM**N**OPQRSTUVWXYZ

nail   A nail is a long, thin piece of metal that can be hammered into wood.

Prairie Dawn is making a wagon.

This **nail** will hold two pieces of my wagon together.

nail   Your nails are the hard coverings that grow on the ends of your fingers and toes.

Biff is cutting his **nails.**

name   A name is the word you use for a person, place, or thing.

Hi! My **name** is Miss Muffet. This is my pet spider. His **name** is Stanley.

nap   When you take a nap, you sleep for a small amount of time.

Snuffle-upagus is taking a **nap.**

narrow   Narrow means not wide.

Sully, that board is too **narrow.** Find one that's wider.

near   Near means close to.

Marshal Grover is **near** the cactus. Fred is far away.

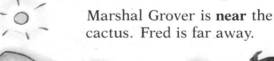

neat Neat means not messy.
Ernie's closet is messy.
Bert's closet is **neat.**

neck Your neck is
the part of your body
between your head
and your shoulders.
Look up the word body.

need When you need something, you
cannot do without it.

needle A needle is a long, thin tool used
for sewing. A needle has a small hole at one
end and a sharp point at the other.

Super Grover **needs** a **needle** and thread to
sew up a hole in his cape.

neighbor A neighbor is someone who lives near you.

neighborhood Your neighborhood is the place where you and your neighbors live.

nephew   If you are a boy, you are your aunt and uncle's nephew.

She is my aunt. He is my uncle.

He is our **nephew.**

nest   A nest is a thing made by birds or other animals to hold their babies.

A baby bird must learn to fly before it leaves its **nest.**

never   Never means not at any time.

If you want to be a grouch like me, you must **never** forget the Grouch Rules.

GROUCH RULES

NEVER SMILE.

NEVER DO ANYTHING THAT IS HELPFUL.

NEVER SAY ANYTHING THAT IS PLEASANT.

new   When something is new, it has just been made or has never been used.

Goldilocks broke Baby Bear's chair.

CRUNCH!

Papa Bear made Baby Bear a **new** chair.

newspaper   A newspaper is one or more sheets of paper printed to tell about the new things that have happened.

Did you hear the **news**? Sherlock Hemlock found a needle in a haystack.

Yes, I read about it in the **newspaper.**

NEWS

SHERLOCK HEMLOCK FINDS PROVERBIAL NEEDLE IN HAYSTACK!

next Next means nearest to or beside.

next Next also means the following one.

Betty Lou is standing **next** to Farley.

We missed the bus. We'll have to take the **next** one.

nice Something that is nice is pleasing.

Everyone likes Barkley because he is a **nice** dog.

nickel A nickel is a coin. A nickel is worth five cents. Look up the word coin.

Each of the Busby twins has five cents.

I have a **nickel**.

I have five pennies.

nickname A nickname is a special name that you use in place of a real name.

His real name is the Amazing Mumford, but I call him Mumphie.

Mumphie is my **nickname**.

niece If you are a girl, you are your aunt and uncle's niece.

She is my aunt. He is my uncle.

She is our **niece**.

night Night is the time of day when it is dark. Night starts when the sun sets and ends when it rises.

Grover sleeps with his teddy bear every **night**.

The Count's Night Poem

Twinkle, twinkle, little stars,
I'd like to put you all in jars.
You'd make the most attractive light
And I could count you every night.

nine   Nine is a number.
Nine is one more than eight.

The Count has **nine**
candles on his piano.

nineteen   Nineteen is a number. Nineteen is ten plus nine more.

Bert has ten Figgy Fizz bottle caps and nine Prune Crush bottle caps in his collection. He has **nineteen** bottle caps all together.

no   No means not true or wrong. No also means you will not or cannot do something. No can also mean not any.

Is your name Goldilocks?

No!

Hey, Bert, do you want to play football?

No!

Do you have any bananas?

No. I have **no** bananas today.

noise   Noise is sound that is not pleasing to hear.

He is making a loud **noise**!

RAT-A-TAT-TAT!

none   None means not any.

There were three bats in my belfry. They all flew away. Now there are **none**.

noon Noon is the middle of the day.
At noon it is twelve o'clock.

It is **noon.** The twelve o'clock train is on time.

nose Your nose is a part of your face. You use your nose to breathe and smell. Look up the word face.

Grover is smelling a flower with his **nose.**

I love flowers. They smell so nice.

nothing Nothing means not anything.

As you can see, there is **nothing** in my hat.

not Not means in no way.

I love stinkweed. Stinkweed does **not** smell nice. It smells terrible. That is why I love it.

now Now means at this time

Do you want to go out to play, Bert?

Not **now,** Ernie. I'll play later.

number A number tells how many.

I have two plates.

I have two carrots.

I have two kittens.

Each monster has the same **number** of things.

nurse A nurse is someone who takes care of people when they are sick.

Farley went to the school **nurse**. He took Farley's temperature.

nut A nut is a dry fruit or seed that is covered by a hard shell.

Walnut   Pecan   Almond

Cashew   Chestnut

Pistachio   Coconut

Oscar, here is my favorite kind of food that begins with the letter N—**nuts**!

And here is my favorite kind of garbage that begins with the letter N—**nut**shells.

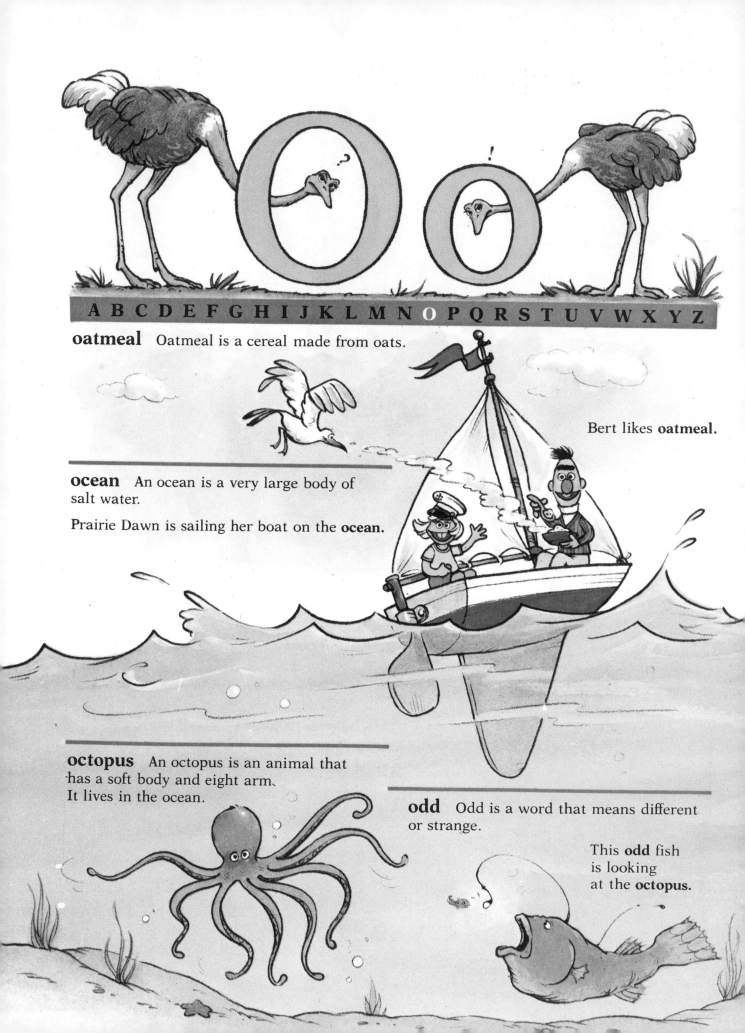

O o

A B C D E F G H I J K L M N **O** P Q R S T U V W X Y Z

oatmeal Oatmeal is a cereal made from oats.

Bert likes **oatmeal.**

ocean An ocean is a very large body of salt water.

Prairie Dawn is sailing her boat on the **ocean.**

octopus An octopus is an animal that has a soft body and eight arm.
It lives in the ocean.

odd Odd is a word that means different or strange.

This **odd** fish is looking at the **octopus.**

of   Of means coming from or belonging to.

Half **of** the pie is missing.

of   Of also means containing or made from.

I have a loaf **of** bread, a jar **of** peanut butter, and a bottle **of** milk for our picnic. What do you have, Ernie?

I have this sign, Bert.

KEEP OFF THE GRASS

off   Off means not on.

off   Off also means not in use.

Ernie, you can turn **off** the radio. The Pigeon News is over.

office   An office is a place where people work.

Farley's mother is president of the Tick Tock Clock Company. She is working in her **office.**

Mommy, do you know what time it is?

PRESIDENT

often   Often means again and again.

Herry Monster **often** breaks things.

I can't help it.

old   When something is old, it is not new.

How do you like these **old** rags?

Old also means how long someone has lived. I am five years **old**.

on   On means touching or covering.

Marshal Grover is **on** his horse, Fred.

on   On also means not turned off.

Shhh, Ernie. I'm listening to the radio. The Pigeon News is **on.**

once   Once means one time.

Woof!

How many times did Barkley bark?

He barked **once.**

one   One is a number. When you count, you begin with the number one.

1 ... **one** Cookie Monster!

only   Only means by itself or no more than.

There is **only** one Cookie Monster.

Thank goodness! This is my **only** cookie.

open   Open means not closed.

The door is **open.**

open   When you open something, you uncover, unfold, unlock, or remove a part of it.

Ernie had to **open** his door...so he could **open** his mailbox...so he could **open** his letter.

opposite   Two things that are opposite are as different from each other as they can be.

Big is the **opposite** of little.

Little is the **opposite** of big.

We are sitting **opposite** each other.

Opposite also means on the other side of.

or   Or means one but not the other.

orange   An orange is a round fruit that grows on an orange tree.

Farley, do you want a grapefruit or an **orange**?

I want an **orange.**

Orange is also the name of a color.

Look up the word color.

orchestra Most orchestras have string, woodwind, brass, and percussion instruments.

cymbals

kettledrums

Percussion

Brass

trombone

tuba

snare drum

piano

French horn

Woodwind

oboe

bassoon

flute

orchestra conductor

trumpet

clarinet

String

cello

baton

sheet music

bass

violin

viola

podium

orchestra conductor   The orchestra conductor is the person who leads the musicians.

The Amazing Mumford is the **orchestra conductor.**

ostrich   The ostrich is the largest bird in the world. It cannot fly but can run very fast.

other   Other means not the same as the one being talked about.

our   Our means belonging to us.

out   When something is out, it is not in.

Betty Lou is in the cannon!

Betty Lou is **out** of the cannon!

outdoors   When you are outdoors, you are not in a building.

Ernie is **outdoors.**

Bert is indoors.

outside   Outside means not inside.

What are you doing **outside** your nest?

I'm painting the **outside** of my nest today.

oven   An oven is a closed space where things can be baked. An oven can be part of a stove.

Cookie the baker bakes bread in an **oven.**

over   Over means above.

The Amazing Mumford waves his magic wand **over** his hat.

---

over   Over also means again.

The trick didn't work, Mumphie. Do it **over.**

over   Over also means the other side up.

If you don't turn your hat **over**, Mumphie, nothing can come out.

over   Over also means finished.

The Amazing Mumford's magic show is **over.**

own   When you own something, or something is your own, it belongs to you.

I **own** two broken umbrellas. Aren't they wonderful?

There is only one great O word. Can you guess what it is?

P p

package   A package is a bundle or a box with something inside. Sometimes a package is wrapped in paper and taped or tied with string.

Hey, Bert, here's a **package** for you!

Nifty, Ernie! My pigeon T-shirt finally came.

page   A page is a piece of paper in a book, a magazine, or a newspaper.

Everything I've ever wanted to know about pigeons is in this book, Bert.

But, Ernie— the **pages** in that book have nothing on them.

That's right, Bert. That's all I want to know about pigeons— nothing! Hee hee hee.

paint   Paint is used to color or protect things. Paint is wet when you put it on something, and then it dries.

Biff and Sully are using green **paint** on the wall.

pair   A pair is two things that go together.

Bert has a **pair** of gloves, a **pair** of Argyle socks, and a **pair** of saddle shoes on the clothesline.

pajamas   Pajamas are clothes to sleep in.

Prairie Dawn is ready for bed. She is wearing her **pajamas.**

YAWN

pal   A pal is a good friend.

pants   A pair of pants is clothing you wear over your hips and legs.

Bert cannot decide which pair of **pants** to wear.

paper   Paper is flat and thin and is used to write and paint on. Paper is also used for wrapping packages and covering walls.

Three of these things belong together. One of these things is not the same.

The **paper** airplane, the news**paper,** and the magazine are made out of **paper.** The frying pan is made out of metal. The frying pan does not belong.

palace   A palace is a very large and fancy house.

Prince Charming lives in a **palace.**

pan   A pan is a metal or glass dish that is used for cooking.

Cookie Monster is frying an egg in a **pan.**

parade   A parade is a group of people who are marching together—usually to music.

What is blue and red and purple and green and comes down the street making a lot of noise?

The Monster Day **parade!**

parent   A parent is a mother or a father.

I'm her mother.

I'm her father.

They are my **parents.**

park   A park is a place outdoors where people can have fun. Sometimes a park has a playground in it.

Bert likes to feed the pigeons in the **park.**

part   When you have a part of something you have some but not all.

I have a whole apple.

Now I have **part** of an apple.

YUM!

party   A party is a group of people having fun together.

Hi, Oscar! I'm on my way to a birthday **party.**

Ugh! Birthday **parties** are no fun. Why don't you stay for my mud **party**?

pass   When you pass something, you go by it.

We **pass** Mr. Hooper's store on our way to school.

HOOPER'S STORE

paste Paste is something you use to make things stick together.

I am using **paste** to **paste** these pictures into my scrapbook.

pat When you pat something, you touch it gently.

PAT THE DOG, PLEASE!

patch A patch is a piece of cloth or other material that is used to cover a tear or a hole.

There is a **patch** on Super Grover's cape.

path A path is a narrow trail that people or animals walk on.

Little Red Riding Hood is walking on the **path** to grandmother's house.

GRANNY'S

pay When you pay for something, you give money for it.

I will **pay** you fifty pennies for sweeping the floor.

Then I will **pay** you fifty pennies for a new bag of marbles.

MARBLES   MARBLES

MARBLES 50¢

MARBLES

pea   A pea is a little, round green vegetable. Peas grow in pods on vines.

peach   A peach is a round fruit with fuzzy skin and a pit in the middle. Peaches grow on peach trees.

peanut   A peanut is a vegetable that grows under the ground. The seed inside the shell is good to eat.

pear   A pear is a fruit with smooth skin. Pears grow on pear trees.

pebble A pebble is a small stone. A pebble is usually smooth and round.

This **pebble** will be great for my **pebble** collection.

peek When you peek at something, you look quickly.

Get ready! I am going to let you **peek** at Slimey.

pen A pen is a tool used for writing or drawing with ink.

I can write my name with a **pen.**

pencil A pencil is a tool used for writing or drawing. A pencil mark can be erased.

I can write my name with a **pencil.**

penny A penny is a coin. A penny is worth one cent. Look up the word coin.

I have six **pennies.**

I have one nickel and one **penny.**

Each of the Busby twins has six cents.

people Children, women, and men are people.
These are some of the **people** in Big Bird's neighborhood.

perfect When something is perfect, it cannot be better.

Sam the robot makes mistakes. Sam is not **perfect.**

person A person is a child, a woman, or a man.

pet A pet is an animal that is loved by the person who takes care of it.

photograph A photograph is a picture taken with a camera. The person who takes the picture is called a photographer.

The **photographer** is taking a **photograph** of Bert and his **pet,** Bernice.

piano A piano is a musical instrument with white and black keys that you press with your fingers.

Don Music is playing the **piano.**

pick When you pick something, you pull it away with your fingers.

Betty Lou likes to **pick** flowers.

pick Pick also means choose.

picnic A picnic is a meal that is eaten outdoors.

I brought my favorite food to the Grouch Day **picnic**— sardines with chocolate sauce.

GROUCH DAY PICNIC

picture A picture shows how something looks. A picture can be a photograph, a painting, or a drawing.

This is a **picture** of me when I was a baby.

pie A pie is something to eat. Most pies are round and have a crust on the outside and a filling on the inside.

What does Frazzle Monster like to put in his **pies**?

His teeth!

GRUNT! GRUNT! SLURP!

piece A piece is one part of something.

I want a **piece** of pie.

pig A pig is an animal with four legs, a short nose called a snout, and a curly tail.

Farmer Grover is feeding his **pigs.**

I am a baby **pig.** I am called a **pig**let.

I am the **pig**let's mother. I am a sow.

I am the **pig**let's father. I am a boar.

pigeon A pigeon is a bird with a small head, a chubby body, and short legs.

Bert loves his **pigeon,** Bernice. Bernice loves Bert.

pile A pile is a group of things lying on top of each other.

Here is a **pile** of dirty laundry. I will wash it.

Here is a **pile** of clean laundry. I will fold it.

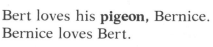

pillow   A pillow is a bag filled with something soft. You can rest your head on a pillow.

pilot   A pilot is someone who flies an airplane. A pilot is also someone who steers a ship.

place   When you know where, you know the place.

pin   A pin is a short, thin piece of metal used to fasten things together.

plain   Something that is plain is not fancy or decorated.

plan   When you plan, you decide what you are going to do before you do it.

plant   A plant is any living thing that is not an animal. Trees, flowers, and grass are kinds of plants.

plant   When you plant a seed, you put it in dirt.

plate   A plate is a flat dish.

play When you play, you do something that is fun.

Big Bird likes to **play** hide-and-seek with Snuffle-upagus.

play When you play a musical instrument, you make music.

Bert likes to **play** his accordion.

play A play is a story that is acted on the stage.

The Sesame Street **Players** are performing a **play.**

please Please is a friendly word to use when you ask someone to do something for you.

plenty When you have all that you need, you have plenty.

plum   A plum is a small, round fruit with smooth skin and a pit in the middle. Plums grow on plum trees.

These **plums** are ripe. They look yummy.

plumber   A plumber is someone who knows how to fix the water and gas pipes in a building.

The **plumber** came to Farley's house to fix the kitchen sink.

plus   Plus means added to.

Two **plus** one is three.

$$\begin{array}{r} 2 \\ +\,1 \\ \hline 3 \end{array}$$

pocket   A pocket is a place in your clothes where you can put things.

Prairie Dawn likes to keep her pet lizard in her **pocket.**

poem   A poem is a special way of saying something. Many poems rhyme.

Mary had a little lamb. Its fleece was white as snow. And everywhere that Mary went, the lamb was sure to go.

point A point is the sharp end of something.

The witch's hat has a **point.**

point When something points, it shows the way.

This sign **points** to the cave of Mr. Snuffle-upagus.

TO THE CAVE OF MISTER SNUFFLE-UPAGUS

poison Poison is something you should not eat or drink because it can make you sick or can kill you.

When I see one of these pictures on something, I know it means **poison,** and I should stay away.

pole A pole is a long, narrow piece of wood or metal.

Oops!

Grover is painting the flag**pole.**

police officer A police officer is a person whose job is to make sure people obey laws.

Mr. **Police Officer,** can you tell me how to get to Sesame Street?

Sure. Right after I give you a ticket for not stopping at that red light.

pond A pond is a small body of water. A pond is bigger than a puddle and smaller than a lake.

Farmer Grover likes to swim in the **pond** with his ducks.

pony A pony is a small horse.

Prairie Dawn likes to ride her **pony.**

pool A pool is a pond or a special place made for people to swim in.

Betty Lou likes to dive into the swimming **pool.**

poor Poor means not having enough money to buy the things you need.

I always send birdseed to my cousin Bartholomew because he is too **poor** to buy it for himself.

poor Poor also means unlucky or unhappy.

Poor Bert. He is all out of oatmeal.

popcorn Popcorn is a special kind of corn that pops when it is heated.

The Count is popping **popcorn.**

... four hundred and ninety-three ... four hundred and ninety-four ... Oh, I love to count the pops!

porcupine A porcupine is a small animal covered with stiff, sharp hairs called quills.

I wonder why some people say that a **porcupine** is like a big pin cushion.

Oh!

possible When something is possible, it can be done.

Is it **possible** that someone brave and smart and strong will hear us calling for help and come to our rescue?

It is **possible.** I can help them.

post office A post office is a place where people can buy stamps, mail letters and packages, and pick up their mail.

Marshal Grover went into the **post office** to mail a letter to his mother.

pot A pot is a deep, round container. Some pots are for cooking and some are for planting flowers in.

Oscar is growing stinkweed in a flower**pot**.

potato A potato is a vegetable that grows in the ground.

Farmer Grover is digging up a **potato** for his dinner.

Farmer Grover is baking the **potato** in the oven.

pour When you pour something, it flows from a container.

power Power is energy or strength to do something.

Pour me another glass of milk, Sam!

It gives me **power** to ride and rope.

practice When you practice, you do something over and over until you can do it better.

Big Bird is learning to use a lasso. He needs to **practice** more.

present   A present is something nice you give to someone for a special reason.

Granny Grouch sent me a **present** for my birthday. I hate **presents.**

Hey, great! It's just what I wanted. A banana peel! Granny Grouch always picks the right color, too. Heh, heh.

pretend   When you pretend, you make believe or imagine.

Bert, you **pretend** to be Little Bo Peep and I'll be your sheep.

You look silly in that sheep costume, Ernie.

pretty   When something is pretty, it is pleasing to look at.

price   The price of something is how much it costs.

Pamela Monster is trying on a **pretty** hat.

What is the **price** of this hat?

prince   A prince is the son of a king and a queen.

princess   A princess is the daughter of a king and a queen.

I am the king.

I am the queen.

I am the **princess.**

I am the **prince.**

prize   A prize is a reward for winning or doing something.

Cookie the baker won a **prize** for the best cookie.

Your cookie is delicious!

Your **prize** is delicious!

problem   A problem is something that is difficult to do or a question that is hard to answer.

How will I get out of here?

Biff has a **problem.**

promise   When you promise to do something, you agree to do it.

I **promise** to take good care of your plants while you are away.

protect   When you protect someone, you keep danger away.

Don't worry! I will **protect** you.

proud   When you feel proud, you feel good about yourself.

When I help people, I feel **proud.**

pudding   Pudding is a soft cooked food. It is usually sweet and is eaten as a dessert.

Mr. Smith wants **pudding** for dessert.

I'll have rice **pudding** …

No, I'll have bread **pudding** …

No, I'll have chocolate **pudding** …

No, I'll have tapioca **pudding** …

puddle   A puddle is a small pool of water on the ground.

Big Bird likes to step in **puddles** when he is wearing his boots.

pull When you pull something, you take hold of it and move it toward you.

Farmer Grover is trying to **pull** his mule into the barn.

push When you push something, you make it move away from you.

Betty Lou is trying to **push** Farmer Grover's mule into the barn.

puppet A puppet is a doll that moves when you pull its strings or put it on your hand.

I want you to meet my **puppets**, Crummy and Yucchy.

put When you put a thing somewhere, you place it there.

Mr. Chatterly is going to **put** his chair next to the fireplace.

puzzle A puzzle is a toy with pieces that fit together.

This is my favorite **puzzle.**

puppy A puppy is a young dog.

The **puppy** is following its mother.

It's no picnic being in this dictionary! I have to put up with all those dumb words like party, play, please, present, and pretty. I can't stand it!

The **Princess** and the **P**

A Funny Fairy Tale
about the Letter **P**

Once upon a time
there was a **princess**
named **Penelope.** One
day **Penelope** was
picking posies in the
park when it began to
pour. She walked and
walked, but she
couldn't find the **path**
back to her **palace.**
And the rain **poured**
and **poured. Poor
Penelope** was dripping
wet and lost.

Suddenly she saw a **pretty palace.** But it was not her
palace. "I wonder who lives in this **place,**" she thought. So
she walked up to the **palace** and **pounded** on the door.

At last the door opened, and standing there was a king and
a queen. They were the **parents** of **Prince Paul.**

"Who are you?" they asked.

"I am **Princess Penelope,**" she said.

The king and queen were looking for a **person** who could
teach **Prince Paul** how to **play** the **piano.** But only a real
princess would do.

"Can you **play** the **piano**?" they asked **Penelope.**

"**Perfectly,**" she answered.

Then the king whispered something to the queen, who said,
"A real **princess** wouldn't be out in the **pouring** rain. You
are just **pretending** to be a **princess.**"

"I **promise** I'm a real **princess,** and I'll do anything to **prove** it," pleaded **Penelope.**

The king and queen began whispering again. Then the queen smiled at **Penelope** and asked her to come in.

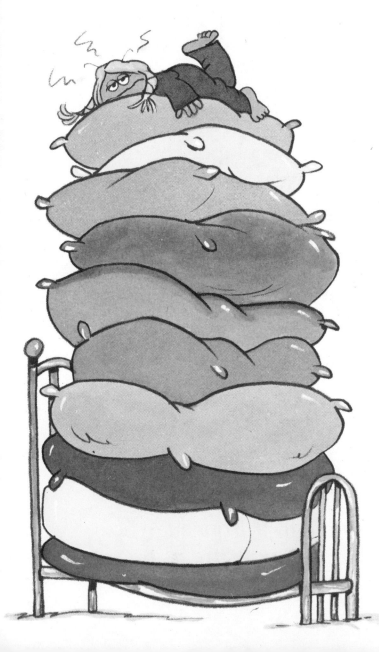

"All right, you can sleep here tonight, but tomorrow you will have to **prove** that you are a **princess,**" said the queen.

She gave **Penelope** a **pair** of **Prince Paul**'s **purple pajamas** and went upstairs to **prepare** a bed for the **princess.** The queen put a big **pile** of **pillows** on the bed. Then she **pulled** a tiny **P** out of her **pocket** and **put** it under the **pile** of **pillows.**

"Your bed is ready, **Princess Penelope,**" the queen called.

The next morning the king and queen asked **Penelope** how she had slept.

"**Poorly!**" said **Penelope.** "Is it **possible** that you **put** a **P** under my **pillow**?"

The queen rushed to **Penelope** and gave her a big hug. "Oh, **Princess Penelope,**" she said, "you *are* a real **princess!**"

The king kissed **Princess Penelope.** "Now, my little **princess,**" he said, "you can teach **Prince Paul** how to **play** the **piano.**" And he led her to the royal music room.

Prince Paul was sitting in the corner **playing** with his collection of **pigeon** feathers.

"Come, **Prince Paul,**" said the king. "We have found a real **princess,** and now she will give you a **piano** lesson."

Prince Paul did not want to **play** the **piano.** He just wanted to **play** with his **pigeon** feathers. But when the **princess** told him to start **playing** the **piano,** he did.

The **princess played** the **piano perfectly,** and soon **Prince Paul** was **playing** almost **perfectly.** The king and queen watched happily.

After **Prince Paul**'s **piano** lesson, the **princess** said, "One thing is **puzzling** me. Why do you need a real **princess** to teach **Prince Paul** how to **play** the **piano?**"

"Because," said the queen, "only a real **princess** can order **Prince Paul** to **practice!**"

So every day **Princess Penelope** came to **Prince Paul**'s **palace,** and every day **Prince Paul practiced playing** the **piano.** Soon he **played perfectly.** And to thank **Princess Penelope,** the king and queen gave her a **pretty purple P** on a necklace, which she wore happily ever after.

Q q

A B C D E F G H I J K L M N O P **Q** R S T U V W X Y Z

quarter A quarter is a coin. A quarter is worth twenty-five cents. Look up the word coin.

Each of the Busby twins has twenty-five cents.

I have a **quarter.**

I have twenty-five pennies.

quarter A quarter is one of four equal parts of something.

Zounds! A **quarter** of the pie is missing!

queen A queen is a woman who rules a country. A queen can also be the wife of a king.

The **queen** is sitting on her throne.

I proclaim today National Be Kind to Grouches Day!

Aaggh!

question A question is what you ask when you want to know something.

Do you have any sardine ice cream with pickles?

The answer to that **question** is no.

quick Quick means fast.

That brown fox is **quick.**

quiet It is quiet when there is no noise.

At last it is **quiet** and I can get some sleep.

The Q section went quickly— but not quickly enough. I have just one question.

When are you going to turn the page so I can quit looking at you?

PARADE TODAY!

How many things that start with the letter **O, P,** or **Q** can you find in the fruit and vegetable parade?

My favorite
was my friend
Ollie the Ostrich.
But wait until you meet
my friend Snuffle-upagus
in the next book.

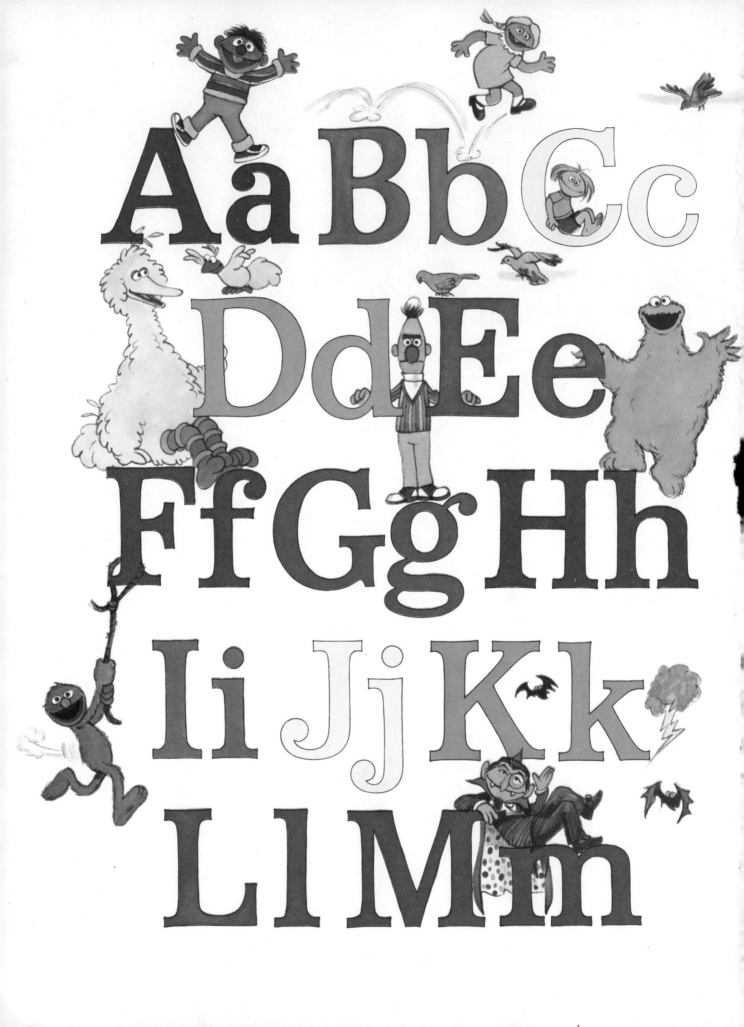